SPICES ON COVER

1. CINNAMON
2. CARAWAY SEEDS
3. TARRAGON
4. BAY LEAF
5. CARDAMOM SEEDS
6. ALLSPICE
7. PEPPER
8. CLOVES
9. CAYENNE PEPPER

The FIRST BOOK of
Spices

by Francine Klagsbrun

ILLUSTRATED BY
PENELOPE NAYLOR

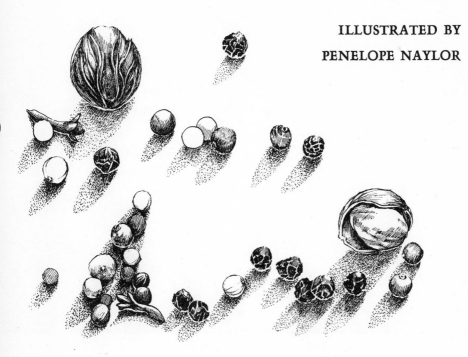

FRANKLIN WATTS, INC.
575 Lexington Avenue, New York, N. Y. 10022

CONTENTS

THE MAGIC OF SPICES

PICK UP a pepper shaker and pour some pepper into your hand. Look at the specks of pepper. They do not sparkle the way a diamond does. They do not glow the way gold does. They do not shine the way silver does.

Yet at one time just a handful of pepper was as valued as a diamond, as sought-after as gold, and as carefully guarded as a sack of silver coins.

That time was long ago. It was more than a thousand years ago, during a period of history known as the Middle Ages. The people of those days lived very differently than we do today. And they ate differently than we do. They did not have a choice of dozens of kinds of meats, fruits, vegetables, and sweets as we have. They did not have huge supermarkets lined with shelves of frozen and canned foods that take only minutes to prepare. They did not even have refrigerators or iceboxes, where food could be stored and preserved.

1

Most of the people of the Middle Ages were peasants who worked the land, raising food for themselves and for the noblemen they served. For the most part, the food that the people raised and ate was dreary and unappetizing. Many of today's vegetables — such as corn and potatoes — were unheard of in Europe. There were no salads to balance a meal, no coffee or tea to finish a dinner, and no chocolate to liven up a dessert.

Worst of all, what little meat the people had to eat usually tasted moldy and spoiled. Nobody knew how to preserve all the hay and grain needed to feed livestock during the long winter months. So, every autumn cattle were slaughtered and the meat salted or pickled so that it could be kept and used throughout the winter. The salted beef had little flavor to begin with, and by midwinter it usually tasted terrible and had an unpleasant odor.

For the common people, bits of moldy meat and tasteless vegetables were customary fare, and few ever expected or demanded more. But the noblemen and wealthy landowners were more fortunate. They had a way out. It was a wonderful, almost magical, way to make mealtimes enjoyable. That way was with spices. By cooking with pepper, cinnamon, nutmeg, cloves, ginger, and other strong spices, the rich people of the Middle Ages managed to hide the odor and taste of moldy meat and to turn dreary soups and vegetables into tempting treats.

Because spices were so costly and hard to get, only the rich could enjoy them. Spices are the dried parts of certain plants — the roots, leaves, seeds, or barks. The people could grow a few spice plants, such as basil or sage, in their gardens. But the best spices and the ones that gave the strongest flavor to foods, such as pepper and cinnamon, came from far-off lands in the East. Few persons knew exactly where those lands were. Some claimed that spices grew on trees near the banks of Paradise and that when they fell off the trees they were washed down a river leading into Egypt. Others insisted

2

that spices flourished in enchanted lands guarded by huge birds and dragons.

Europeans did not dare to enter the mysterious lands of the East. Instead, they relied on Arab traders for their spices. Somehow — and most persons did not know how — Arab caravans brought the spices from the East to Egypt. From there, the dried roots, leaves, seeds, and barks were shipped to European seaports to be sold in the marketplaces. By the time the spices reached the people, the prices were sky-high.

During the early days of the Middle Ages only the richest and most powerful nobles could afford the luxury of spices. As time went on and trade increased, more and more spices were brought into Europe and more persons were able to buy them. Still, spices remained among the most precious of all possessions. In some places, a pound of ginger was worth as much as a sheep. In others, a person could buy three sheep or half a cow with a pound of mace. Pepper — always the most valuable of all spices — was used as money for paying rent and taxes. In England, the guards on the docks of London, where ships unloaded spices, were forced to sew up their pockets to make sure they did not steal even a single peppercorn.

For hundreds of years, spices were symbols of wealth and power. Then, in the 1300's and 1400's, a new age began in Europe. It was the Age of Discovery, when people set out to learn as much as possible about the world around them. Adventurous men became fascinated with the mystery and magic of spices. They no longer felt frightened by stories of monsters and dragons. They no longer felt content to allow Arab merchants to control the profitable spice trade. They determined to find the far-off spice lands on their own, to win glory for their homeland and wealth and honor for themselves.

And so the search was on, first for new land routes to the East

SPICES AND COUNTRIES

ALLSPICE
Jamaica

ANISE
Egypt
Spain
Syria
Turkey

BASIL
Belgium
France
Hungary
India
Iran

BAY LEAF
Greece
Portugal
Turkey
Yugoslavia

CARAWAY SEED
Denmark
Lebanon
The Netherlands
Turkey

CAYENNE PEPPER
United States

CELERY SEED
France
India

CHERVIL
France

CHILI POWDER
United States

CINNAMON
Ceylon
Indonesia
South Vietnam

CLOVES
Madagascar
Zanzibar

CORIANDER
Argentina
France
Morocco
Romania

CUMIN SEED
Iran
Lebanon
Morocco
Syria

CURRY POWDER
India

DILL
India
United States

FENNEL
Argentina
India

GINGER
India
Jamaica

MARJORAM
Greece
Lebanon
United States

MINT
Belgium
France
Germany
United States

MUSTARD
Canada
Denmark
Great Britain
United States

NUTMEG AND MACE
Indonesia

OREGANO
Italy

PAPRIKA
Hungary

PEPPER
Brazil
Ceylon
India
Indonesia

POPPY SEED
Denmark
The Netherlands
Poland
Sweden
Turkey

ROSEMARY
Portugal
Spain
United States

SAFFRON
Portugal
Spain

SAGE
Greece
United States
Yugoslavia

SAVORY
France
Spain

TARRAGON
France
United States
Yugoslavia

THYME
France
Portugal
Spain

TURMERIC
Haiti
India
Jamaica
Peru

CANADA

UNITED STATES

HAITI

JAMAICA

PERU

BRAZIL

ARGENTINA

and then for more direct water routes. One by one the leading nations of Europe sent their bravest navigators to find the shortest possible water routes to India and other eastern spice lands. And one by one men such as Christopher Columbus, Vasco da Gama, and Ferdinand Magellan set out on their search for spices. They did not all succeed. Columbus never reached the Orient, and Magellan was killed before his fleet's voyage ended. But the treasures these men discovered during their journeys were far greater even than the valuable spices they had set out to find. What began as a search for spice lands ended in the discovery and exploration of a new world.

Look again at the pepper in your hand. It might not sparkle or glow or shine. But it stands for a story of adventure and glory, a story of conquest and bravery that changed the course of the world.

CARAVANS FROM THE EAST

THE BOY trembled. It was dark and damp in the pit where he lay, and he was frightened. A little earlier his brothers had stripped him of his beautiful colored robe and thrown him into the empty pit. What would they do with him now? Murder him and leave his body to the wild animals? Or would they just abandon him, to die slowly of hunger and thirst?

Nearby his brothers sat together eating and talking. They knew they must somehow rid themselves of this pesky younger brother who had become their father's pet. But how?

Suddenly, in the distance, they saw what looked like a long black line moving slowly toward them. A caravan! As it approached, they could hear the rough voices of the camel drivers urging their animals on, and they could see swarthy Arab merchants dressed in turbans and long robes.

The brothers had seen similar caravans many times before. They were caravans of Ishmaelites, or Arabs, that made their way from distant eastern lands, across hot desert sands and rugged wilderness until they reached the land of Egypt. Sometimes there were thousands of camels in a caravan, each laden with packs of spices and silks from the East.

Here was their answer.

"Come, let us sell him to the Ishmaelites," said one of the brothers.

The others agreed. It was a good way to get rid of their young brother without shedding his blood. As the caravan approached, they quickly lifted the boy from the pit, and for twenty pieces of silver sold him into slavery to the Arab merchants.

The boy's name was Joseph, and the story of how his brothers sold him to a caravan of Arab merchants is told in the Book of Genesis in the Bible. The time in which Joseph lived was thousands of years before the Middle Ages, thousands of years before there was a Europe such as we know. But already in those ancient days, people had discovered the wonders of spices. Even in those early times, a brisk trade was carried on between the Far Eastern lands where spices grew and the countries farther to the west.

Arab merchants, such as the Ishmaelites who carried Joseph away, were the go-betweens in the spice trade. They bought their spices in port cities of India, mostly from Indian and Chinese traders. Then they loaded their treasures onto camels and began the long overland trek westward to the marketplaces of Babylonia, Assyria, and Egypt. Their journeys were slow and dangerous. Pirates waited to attack them in unprotected areas. Kings and rulers demanded heavy tolls as the caravans passed through their lands. But the Arab merchants also managed to trade with the peoples along the way, selling their spices for gold and silver and buying goods and slaves to sell in the marketplaces toward which they headed.

The Arabs were clever. They knew that they could control the spice trade so long as nobody found out just where their precious merchandise came from. So they made up frightening stories about the lands in which the spices grew. Because travel was slow in those days and there was no easy way for most people to reach the true sources of spices, they did not find it hard to accept the Arab tales of horror. In fact, for thousands of years those tales continued to frighten Europeans and to ensure the Arabs a complete hold on the spice trade.

Whether or not the ancient peoples knew the sources, they did know the value of spices. The ancient Egyptians burned spices as part of their religious ceremonies and used spice oils in embalming the bodies of their rulers. The ancient Assyrians believed that their gods drank a special spiced wine made of sesame seeds. One of the earliest Assyrian writings describes the gods drinking sesame-seed wine at a meeting held just before they created the earth.

The ancient Hebrews used spices in cooking and in making anointing oils and perfumes. The Bible tells how King Solomon traded in spices with the Phoenicians and other neighboring peoples. And when the beautiful Queen of Sheba came to visit the rich and famous king, she brought him gold and precious stones and "camels bearing spices."

The ancient Phoenicians grew rich from spices. For almost 400 years, from about 1200 to 800 B.C., their city of Tyre served as a major port of the Mediterranean Sea. Excellent sailors and traders, the Phoenicians distributed to cities along the Mediterranean coast the spices brought to Tyre by Arab caravans.

Egyptians, Phoenicians, Babylonians, Assyrians — one by one different peoples rose and fell from power in ancient times. But through the centuries, the long caravans of Arabs continued to make their way over familiar trade routes, carrying their cargoes of oriental spices to hungry marketplaces in the West. When the ancient Greeks and Romans had their turn in power, it was the Arabs who remained their suppliers of those treasured goods.

THE GREEKS AND ROMANS

OF ALL the ancient peoples, the Greeks and Romans probably used the most spices. The odor of spices made them especially important in Greek religious ceremonies. The Greeks, who worshiped many gods, often honored those gods in their temples by burning incense made of a mixture of spices. The Greek name for spices was *aroma*. From this name comes our word for spicy odor or fragrance.

The Romans conquered the Greeks and built a mighty empire that included most of the known world at that time. As the wealth of the empire increased, so did the love of luxuries. The Romans used pounds and pounds of spices and willingly paid the high prices asked for them. A favorite Roman treat was spice cake made with cumin, anise, and other spices. Like the Greeks, the Romans used spices in religious ceremonies. They also burned spices as a sign of honor at funerals. Roman historians describe how the cruel emperor Nero murdered his wife in a fit of rage. Then to show how much he had really loved her, he burned an entire year's supply of cinnamon during her funeral ceremony.

Over the years, as Arab merchants continued to grow wealthy from the spice trade, Roman rulers became eager to find the source of the precious item. The Romans had some idea about India and the other eastern lands that spices came from. But they did not know the routes the Arabs used to get to and from those lands. The routes had changed during the course of time. In addition to the caravans that slowly plodded overland, Arab ships, filled with spices, now made their way from India, along the coast of southern Arabia, through the Red Sea, and into Egypt. Other routes carried the traders by ship through the Persian Gulf and then overland across northern Arabia to port cities along the coast of the Mediterranean Sea.

In desperation, the first Roman emperor, Augustus, sent an expedition to Arabia to question the Arabs about their secret routes. Because the Arabs feared the Romans, they did give directions. However, they made sure to describe only the longest and most difficult land routes, making the journey so wearing that the Romans gained nothing.

When the Romans set out on their own to find water routes to the East, they were driven back by storms and fierce winds. Finally, in the early days of the Christian era, the Romans learned how to use the monsoons, the seasonal winds that blow across the Indian Ocean. At long last, with the help of these winds, Roman sailing ships were able to cross the Indian Ocean to the marketplaces of India and to return home filled with rich cargoes from the East.

Now the spice trade grew greater than ever. At its center was the city of Alexandria in Egypt. The Romans had conquered Alexandria in 30 B.C. and had made it a chief port for all trade between Europe and Asia. In Alexandria, the Romans built huge warehouses to hold spices, and from there the spices were shipped to cities throughout the empire. Pepper and other spices were such an important part of Alexandria's trade that one entrance to the city was known as the Pepper Gate.

A RANSOM IN SPICES

ONE DAY the trade and conquests and glory ended. For years, fierce tribes of Goths and Huns had roamed Europe attacking various parts of the Roman Empire. Finally, these tribes sapped the strength of the empire and brought it to an end. The Romans called the tribesmen barbarians. Compared to the Romans, the barbarians were uncivilized and uncultured. They knew nothing about literature and the arts or about sports and feasts. But one thing they had learned from the Romans was the value of spices.

In A.D. 410, hordes of barbarians called Visigoths, led by their king, Alaric, swarmed down on the city of Rome. Everywhere they went they destroyed buildings, smashed statues, looted marketplaces, and terrified the people. Now they stood ready to murder the entire population. First, however, Alaric offered his victims a choice. He gave them a way to save their lives — to ransom themselves. His price was gold, silver, silks, and jewels. But most important of all, the people were to give him three thousand pounds of peppercorns and continue to pay him a tribute of three hundred pounds a year.

For the Romans, there was no choice. They had to accept the bargain, difficult as it was to raise the pepper ransom. For awhile they saved themselves from destruction. By the mid-400's, however, even pepper could no longer save Rome. The empire collapsed and many of the people were killed or taken as slaves.

MOSLEMS, CHRISTIANS, AND SPICES

AT FIRST, it was as though darkness had descended upon western Europe. Gone were the mighty Roman armies, the great banquets, the bustling cities. Gone, too, were the flourishing trade routes, the graceful ships laden with spices, the crowded, noisy, colorful marketplaces. Now most men stayed close to home, living off the produce of their own lands, making do with dull, unchanging meals. During the early years of the Middle Ages, for about three hundred years or so after the fall of Rome, the sea routes that the Romans had so carefully followed to the spice markets of India were neglected and forgotten. Few people ever thought about the far-off lands to the East. Fewer still even remembered what spices tasted like.

In the East, however, things were different. There, a new empire was growing, a new religion taking hold, and new and profitable spice trade routes opening up.

A camel driver named Mohammed began it all. Mohammed was born in A.D. 570 in the city of Mecca in northwestern Arabia. As an adult, he came to believe that he was the true prophet of God. Mohammed's Arab followers, known as Moslems, carried his teachings first to Arabia and then throughout Asia and into Europe.

As they spread their religion and ideas, the Moslems also spread the use of spices, in which they had a special interest. As a young man, Mohammed had married a wealthy widow whose husband had been a spice merchant. Mohammed took over his wife's spice business and sought to increase it even while he carried out his religious work. His followers learned from him to combine business interests with religion. Many Moslem missionaries ended up settling along the coast of India and becoming merchants in the spice trade.

In the beginning, the Arabs traded mostly within their eastern empire. As time went on, and trade and commerce revived in western Europe, the Arabs once again became the main link in the spice business. Arab merchants discovered new overland routes to the Far East, and Arab ships made regular voyages to India and China. Just as they had hundreds of years earlier, the Arabs kept their trade routes a dark secret from westerners.

By the 800's and 900's, a taste for spices had been reawakened in western Europe. Beginning in the 1000's, that taste reached new heights. Again, it was religious zeal that spread the story of spices. From the 1000's to the 1200's, Christians throughout Europe set out on Crusades to the East to win the Holy Land from the Moslems. In the process, the Europeans came to taste and love eastern spices that they had barely known existed. When they returned home, they longed for the delicious seasonings that could make their foods so appetizing. As a result, spices became as precious as gold and silver, and Arab and Christian spice merchants built up a flourishing trade.

MIGHTY VENICE

AT THE HEART of the new spice trade was the city of Venice. Beautiful Venice on the northern coast of Italy began as a fishermen's village of huts and shacks. Soon spices, sailors, and daring sea voyages turned the village of huts into the mightiest and wealthiest city in all Europe.

It was Venetian ships that carried armies of Crusaders across the Mediterranean Sea to Syria, Egypt, and Palestine. And it was Venetian ships that came back loaded with spices, silks, jewels, and other eastern treasures to sell in the marketplaces of Europe.

Built on a cluster of islands, over the years Venice had developed a powerful navy. Large docks and shipyards lined the city's coast. And sleek, swift ships, called galleys, stood ready to sail the most dangerous waters.

As Europe's appetite for spices increased, Venice became its spice merchant. Into Venice poured tons of goods — woolens from England, furs from Russia, wines from other cities of Italy. Venetian galleys carried these goods to port cities in Syria and Egypt. There merchants traded the European goods for spices brought by Arab caravans from India and other eastern lands. Laden with spices, the galleys then returned to Venice, and from there the spices were sent by land and sea to cities throughout Europe.

At its height, the Venetian navy had three thousand merchant ships. The day a fleet left on a spice voyage was a special day of celebration in Venice. People dressed in colorful costumes danced and sang in the city square. Noisy parades marched through the city, passing in review before the doge, the ruler of Venice. Solemn church services were held to pray for the safe return of the great fleet.

Everybody gathered to watch and cheer as the fleet set sail. First the flagship — the admiral's ship — took off. Then came a long line of merchant ships carrying their precious cargoes. Following closely were armed warships sent to protect the merchant fleet from pirates and jealous enemy nations.

If you had lived in Venice in those days, you might have imagined yourself to be at the center of the universe. Streaming into your city would have been riverboats and barges and packtrains carrying cargoes from many lands. And everywhere around you would have been beautiful churches, public buildings, and paintings — some of them the greatest the world has ever known, and almost all created under the patronage of merchants made wealthy by spice trading. Never could you have imagined a time when Venice would not reign as the proud, mighty ruler of the Mediterranean.

Yet that time was approaching. In the 1200's, at the very height of Venice's power, the stage was being set for its downfall. Strangely, the person perhaps most responsible was a Venetian himself.

"MARCO MILLIONS"

HIS NAME was Marco Polo. And the story of his adventures helped to overthrow Venice, destroy the Arab hold on the spice trade, and spur the Age of Discovery.

Certainly young Marco could not have foreseen any of those events when he left Venice at the age of seventeen, in the year 1271. He was simply off on a business trip with his father and his uncle. The two older men were jewel merchants. They had already traveled widely through the Near East, and had even gone to China, which they called Cathay. Now they were making a second trip to buy and sell merchandise, and they were taking Marco with them.

The business trip turned into a twenty-four-year journey that took Marco and his family through China, India, and other parts of Asia. The Polos stayed at the court of the Mongol emperor Kublai Khan, and in his service they traveled throughout the Orient.

Marco was forty-one years old when he finally returned to Venice in 1295. Three years later he was taken prisoner in a sea battle between Venice and Genoa. In his prison cell, he dictated the story of his journey to a fellow prisoner, who wrote it on parchment. Later, Marco's story was published as *The Adventures of Marco Polo*.

It was a fascinating book. It told of lands and peoples that no Europeans had ever visited, and few had even heard of. It told of strange religions, of fierce wars inside Asia, and of "peculiar" customs such as the use of paper money.

It also told of spices. Marco Polo was the first European to see and write about the eastern lands where spices grow. He did not find huge monsters and dreadful birds guarding the precious spices, as the Arabs had warned. Instead, he saw beautiful trees, from which cloves, ginger, and cinnamon come, and busy markets "frequented by traders from all parts of India, who bring spices and drugs."

Marco found that the country of Java (part of Indonesia today) "abounds with rich commodities. Pepper, nutmegs . . . cloves and all the other valuable spices and drugs are the produce of the island; which occasion it to be visited by many ships laden with merchandise, that yields to the owners considerable profit."

In the province of Manji, he said, "large quantities of ginger are produced, which are conveyed through all the province of Cathay, with great profit to the merchants."

The province of Tibet, he noted, "produces cloves. The tree is small; the branches and leaves resemble those of the laurel, but are somewhat longer and narrower. Its flowers are white and small, as are the cloves themselves, but as they ripen they become dark-colored."

This was world-shaking information gathered at first hand — and almost nobody believed it. Most people thought Marco's stories were wildly exaggerated. They laughingly nicknamed him "Marco Millions," because of the vast number of spices, jewels, and silks he claimed to have seen.

But there were some persons who did not laugh at Marco Polo. Among them were merchants who saw a new way of life in Marco's adventures. Why could they not travel to the far-off lands of Cathay and India as Marco had done and buy spices directly from the East to bypass Venice and the Arabs?

For awhile they did. Dozens of merchants and missionaries took to the roads, traveling the long overland route to the Orient. Then, in the 1300's, the Mongols, who had been so friendly to Marco Polo and other Europeans, fell from power. The emperors who replaced them had little interest in Europeans and discouraged foreign visitors.

Venice — never really disturbed by Marco's travels — grew mightier than ever, and Arab caravan owners tightened their hold on the spice trade. But "Marco Millions" was not forgotten. As time went on, his book of travels became more and more popular, stirring the imagination of a new generation of adventurous men. Among its most careful readers was a young Italian sea captain named Christopher Columbus.

THE SEARCH IS ON

ONE BURNING question haunted Columbus. Was there no *direct* way to reach the wondrous lands that Marco Polo had described?

For years, Europeans had accepted the idea that the only way to get to and from the East was through a combination of complicated land and sea routes. They had complained about the terribly high prices of spices, about the secretive Arab merchants, about the haughty and wealthy Venetians. For years, they had complained and had done nothing.

Now, almost suddenly, they were ready for a change. Columbus was not the only man to read Marco Polo's travel stories. Nor was he the only man to dream of a new route to the riches of the East. Everywhere during the 1400's, men became caught up in a single idea — to find a direct sea route to India and the spice lands of the Orient.

Columbus differed from the others in one major way. They assumed that the only way to reach the East was to sail east. He decided that the best way to reach the East was to sail west. From Marco Polo's descriptions and from the writings of early geographers, Columbus had become convinced that Asia was an enormous land, separated from Europe by a fairly small body of water — the Atlantic Ocean. By sailing west across the Atlantic, he believed, he could reach Japan and from there go on to India.

Columbus was wrong, of course. The land he reached in 1492 was not an island near Japan as he believed. It was a whole new world.

17

The Atlantic Ocean was much larger than he had guessed, and two continents and another ocean separated Europe from Asia.

But at first nobody knew that. The day Columbus returned from his first voyage was a day of rejoicing in Spain, the country that had supported him and his voyage. "Columbus has discovered the water route to the Indies," people told one another excitedly. "Now Spain will be master of the spice trade." True, Columbus had brought no spices back with him. Still, had he not assured everyone that ". . . precious stones, spices, and a thousand other things may surely be expected now"? Had not his physician, Dr. Chanca, described the sight of a beautiful tree, "whose leaf had the finest smell of cloves I ever met with"?

A SEA ROUTE AT LAST

IN SPAIN, the people rejoiced. In nearby Portugal, they were shocked. For years, tiny Portugal had prepared itself for the all-important sea voyage to India. As early as 1416, its prince, Henry the Navigator, had established a naval college to study ways of improving navigation. Led by Henry, Portuguese shipbuilders had designed new, sturdy ships called caravels. Inspired by Henry, brave Portuguese navigators had set out to explore the west coast of Africa and push farther and farther eastward through waters and passages that Europeans had feared for years.

Was all Henry's work for nothing? Had the Portuguese been wrong in seeking an eastern route to Asia? Had Spain won the race to the East, and with it the valuable prize of spices?

Doubt quickly followed the first feelings of shock. If, indeed, Columbus had reached the Indies through his western route, why had he not brought back many treasures with him? All he had to show for his "great" voyage was crude jewelry and clothing and strange-looking men whom he called Indians. Portugal would not give up that easily. Let the Spaniards sail westward. They, the Portuguese, would continue to make their way eastward, around Africa, until they reached their goal.

They were right. They proved it to the world one September day in 1499, when a battered ship limped into Lisbon Harbor. From the ship stepped the Portuguese navigator Vasco da Gama, glowing with pride. He had lost half his fleet, and two out of every three of his men had died from illness and hardship. But he had accomplished his mission. He had reached India and had brought back enough spices to pay for his voyage sixty times over.

It had been a difficult, almost unbearable, voyage. Da Gama and his men had sailed around the western coast of Africa, past the Cape of Good Hope, and then on to Calicut (now Kozhikode), India.

From the moment they arrived in India they faced trouble. Jealous Arab spice merchants realized that now, at last, their secret had been uncovered. They could no longer frighten away Europeans from the East and the profitable spice trade. They could make things so unpleasant, however, that the foreigners would never return.

Every day, da Gama and his men fell into some difficulty with the Arabs and with the Indians whom the Arabs had turned against them. Sometimes they barely escaped cruel Arab plots to destroy them and their ships. Finally, after three months in Calicut and nearby cities, da Gama decided to return home. But not before he had loaded his ships with nutmegs, cloves, pepper, cinnamon, and ginger. And not before he had received a letter from the ruler of Calicut agreeing to trade peacefully with the Portuguese.

Now, after more than two years, da Gama was home, and Portugal went wild. It was a day of celebration that people would remember for a long time. One man had made a sea voyage, and little Portugal had become a leading world power.

SPAIN VERSUS PORTUGAL

IT WAS a black day in Venice, the day that news came of da Gama's voyage. Almost overnight, that proud city lost its grandeur. Da Gama's expedition proved without doubt that the best way to carry eastern spices to the West was by sea. Suddenly, the old caravan trails and Venice's trade routes in the Mediterranean were useless. Portugal took over as the spice merchant of Europe, and the might and wealth of Venice faded into the past.

Other Portuguese navigators followed da Gama's sea route to the Indies. By the early 1500's, the Portuguese claimed the lands of Ceylon, the East Indies, and finally the Moluccas, or Spice Islands, which are part of Indonesia today. These islands were the source of two of the most valued of all spices — cloves and nutmegs.

The Portuguese were not alone in reaching the Spice Islands. During the early 1500's, the Spanish also found their way there, using a completely different route.

The Spanish had come to realize that Columbus had not reached India at all during his voyages, but had discovered a new land. Although Columbus always insisted that he *had* found a water route to the Indies, people stopped paying attention to him. He had brought back no spices from his "India," and spices were what all the world wanted.

However, the Spanish had not completely given up Columbus' idea of finding a western route to India. When the Portuguese navigator Ferdinand Magellan proposed to find the Spice Islands by sailing westward, King Charles V of Spain quickly agreed to support his trip.

Magellan's search for spices brought about the greatest of all voyages, the first trip around the world. Before that voyage ended, Magellan was killed in the Philippines. Still, he received credit for this

20

daring journey that led across the Atlantic Ocean, around the tip of South America, through the Pacific Ocean, to the Spice Islands, and then back to Spain. The man who did complete the voyage was Sebastián del Cano. On September 8, 1522, he sailed into the harbor of Seville with one leaky ship and a treasure in spices that included twenty-six tons of cloves and large amounts of cinnamon, mace, and nutmegs. As a reward, he received a lifetime pension and a special coat of arms. Its design showed two sticks of cinnamon, three nutmegs, and twelve cloves.

Del Cano's homecoming was just the excuse the Spanish needed to rival the Portuguese in the spice trade. Earlier, in 1494, the pope had drawn an imaginary line through the globe, dividing the world into an eastern and western half. By treaty, Portugal was permitted to trade and claim lands in the eastern half and Spain in the western half. Now each country insisted that the Spice Islands lay within its half, and each claimed sole possession of these rich lands.

They quarreled for seven years. Finally, in 1529, Spain's King Charles V sold his rights to the Spice Islands to his brother-in-law, King John III of Portugal. The Spanish had discovered that Columbus' "worthless" lands contained gold, and they decided to turn their attention there.

Now Portugal held complete control of the spice trade — at least for awhile.

THE DUTCH TAKE OVER

THE PORTUGUESE were so busy with their eastern voyages that they barely had enough time or men left to ship their spices to other countries of Europe. So they often hired Dutch ships to handle their spice business in Europe.

They soon found out that they had made a terrible mistake. The Dutch quickly grew tired of serving as middlemen in the spice trade. Gradually they began sending their own explorers to the Spice Islands and other parts of Southeast Asia. These men made friends with native rulers and organized trading posts throughout the East. In 1602, the Dutch formed a trading company, called the Dutch East India Company, to sponsor expeditions and handle the country's growing spice industry.

Almost before the Portuguese could realize what had happened, they had lost control of the spice trade to Holland. In a series of fierce struggles, the Dutch conquered three key spice lands in the Indian Ocean — Malacca, the Malay Peninsula, and northern Sumatra. Later they took over the cinnamon trade in Ceylon and won

control of the pepper ports along the coast of India. By the end of the 1600's, the Dutch could proudly call themselves masters of the spice trade.

And cruel masters they were. Nothing could stop them from making a profit, even if they had to beat and torture the natives who planted and gathered spices. Once they had gained control of a region, they forbade the people there from trading with any other country. Anyone caught disobeying those orders was instantly put to death.

To keep the price of spices high in Europe, the Dutch burned and uprooted thousands of beautiful spice trees. In that way, they made sure that there was always a shortage of spices, and they could charge as much as they liked. To be absolutely certain that nobody else would plant nutmeg trees outside the area they controlled, the Dutch soaked all nutmegs in lime before shipping them to Europe. They mistakenly believed that the lime killed the germ of the nutmeg so that it could not be replanted and made to grow anyplace else.

THE FRENCH AND THE ENGLISH

WITH ALL their care, the Dutch did not succeed in protecting their spice interests. All their rules and threats could not prevent a clever Frenchman from smuggling precious spices from the Dutch-held Spice Islands and shipping them to French possessions in the Indian Ocean. Nobody knows exactly how the Frenchman, Pierre Poivre, did it. But somehow, shortly after he visited the Dutch islands, there arrived in the French possession of Mauritius seventy clove trees, four hundred nutmeg trees, and thousands of clove and nutmeg seeds ready for planting. The plants flourished in Mauritius and were later sent to other French-held lands in the Indies. Their cultivation marked the beginning of the end of the Dutch monopoly on spices.

Meanwhile, something else was happening that would lead to the downfall of the Dutch spice control. Just as the Portuguese had challenged the Venetians and the Dutch had challenged the Portuguese, now the British challenged the Dutch.

The British had been slow in joining the spice race, but they had always had a deep love for spices. As early as the 1000's, they had formed a trade guild of "Pepperers," or merchants dealing in the pepper trade. During the 1300's, the Pepperers were registered under the Latin name of *grossarii*. The name came from a measurement used in weighing spices, and from it we get our word "grocer." By the 1500's, the British were becoming interested in the spice trade. By the 1600's, they had chartered an East India Company of their own and were rivaling the Dutch for control of spice markets.

For almost two hundred years, until the end of the 1700's, the British and Dutch fought over the spice trade. In the end, Britain won. The British gained control of India itself and took over many of the Dutch possessions in Southeast Asia. Holland declined, as had so many spice powers before it.

Among the thousands of men working for the British East India Company during its years of power was an American named Elihu Yale. During twenty-seven years in India, from 1672 to 1699, he built a fortune in spices. When he returned to America, he donated money and books to a struggling college in Connecticut. It became one of the country's great educational institutions — Yale University. Its founding was just the beginning of the spice adventures of the new little country across the Atlantic.

SALEM'S SAILORS

SOME PEOPLE say that Captain William Vans was the first Yankee captain to make a pepper voyage. Many others claim that Captain

Jonathan Carnes was the true pioneer of the pepper trade in the United States.

Nobody knows for sure. But one thing we do know. At the end of the 1700's, while the Dutch and the British were still fighting over the spice trade, American sea captains made journeys of their own that soon gave them the greatest pepper profit of all.

It all began in the tiny seaport of Salem, Massachusetts. Salem's sea captains had discovered a source of pepper that Europeans had overlooked for years. They found that thousands of pepper trees grew on the mountains in the interior of the island of Sumatra in Southeast Asia. The Europeans had traded along the coast of Sumatra, but had not penetrated the interior of the island.

For good reason. The Malay tribes who lived in Sumatra were fierce, warring people who thought nothing of slaughtering white men. It was a risky business, trying to deal directly with the Malays. There was no guarantee that you would come away with anything, including your life.

But Americans were willing to take the risk. Whether or not Captain Carnes was the first to make the voyage to Sumatra, he certainly caused a sensation in 1796 when he sailed into Salem Harbor with a pepper cargo from Sumatra. The cargo was worth more than one hundred thousand dollars, and brought a 700 per cent profit over what the voyage had cost. After that, nothing could stop American seamen from making similar voyages.

Although American clipper ships sailed from Boston and other New England ports during the early 1800's, Salem became the true center of the pepper trade. It served not only the United States, but the entire world. In 1805, Salem exported more than seven million pounds of pepper to countries throughout the world. In 1818, so much pepper was brought into Salem that the duties collected on it were enough to pay 5 per cent of the expenses of the entire United States government.

Salem's merchants prospered and Salem's sailors became world-known for their courage. Many of Salem's women and children, however, earned nothing but tears and heartaches from the pepper trade. The trip to and from Sumatra covered twenty-four thousand miles and lasted from two to three years. Every step of the journey was filled with danger. On the seas, treacherous pirates waited to pounce on American vessels, to steal their cargoes and murder their crews. On land, savage headhunting tribes stood ready to massacre the first foreigners they saw. A wife, a child, a sweetheart could never be sure that the loved one they had kissed good-bye would return to them.

Many of the stories of death and daring during Salem's pepper voyages were told by crewmen who had survived. One of the best known is the story of the merchant ship *Friendship*.

Captain Charles M. Endicott had left the *Friendship* anchored off the coast of Sumatra while he and some crewmen went ashore to buy pepper. When they returned, they discovered that Malay pirates had swarmed aboard their ship, killing and wounding most of the crew, and stealing whatever they could find. Quickly, the captain and his men rowed to a nearby port. There they found three other American ships, whose captains volunteered to sail back with Endicott and help him retake his ship from the Malays.

As soon as the Malays saw the armed Americans approaching, they abandoned the stolen ship. Endicott and the surviving crew members returned to the United States, where they reported their story to the government. Immediately, the United States Navy was called into action, and the frigate *Potomac* was sent to avenge the bloody piracy against the *Friendship*. The *Potomac* opened fire on the Malay town from which the pirates had come. Its powerful guns killed more than a hundred persons before the Malays raised the flag of truce.

The revenge of the *Friendship* took place in 1831. For almost ten years after that, Salem's pepper trade continued to flourish. Finally, during the 1840's, pirates and the perils of the sea won out. The American government no longer felt that it could send its ships into foreign waters to protect Salem's pepper fleets. In addition, times were changing. Pepper and other spices were easier to come by, now that all their sources were known. Prices were lower, and dangerous pepper voyages brought few profits.

SPICES FOR EVERYONE

TODAY, PEPPER VOYAGES, East India companies, and spice wars are part of the faraway past. Pepper, cinnamon, mace, nutmeg, cardamom seeds, and other spices stand on kitchen shelves everywhere, from New York to Tokyo. They cost only a few cents a jar, and are as close at hand as the neighborhood supermarket.

As the greatest industrial power in the world, the United States leads in the spice industry. Many spices that once grew only in eastern lands are now grown in the United States and its territories. Many other spices are imported from all parts of the world to meet the constant demands of Americans for spices of every kind.

New York City is the spice capital of the nation. To its docks come hundreds of ships carrying boxes and bundles of spices from many lands. The spices have been dried before being shipped, either in the sun or in special drying machines. After the dried spices are unloaded in New York, officials of the Pure Food and Drug Administration inspect them to make sure that they are not spoiled or dangerous to health. Then the spices are placed in big warehouses. Many of these warehouses stand on the lower west side of Manhattan, overlooking the Hudson River.

From the warehouses, the spices are shipped to mills throughout the country. There laboratory workers test them to see that they are pure, and then grade them according to the way they will be used. Next, special grinding machines clean and grind the spices, sometimes into fine grinds and sometimes into coarser grinds, depending on their use. Finally, packaging machines place the ground spices in containers, ready to be shipped to food factories and stores everywhere. A package of spice, such as ginger or nutmeg, may range in size from a one-ounce jar to be sold to a homemaker to a two-hundred-pound sack that will be used by a food manufacturer in making prepared meats or relishes.

Every year Americans use more than two hundred million pounds of spices. That number may seem enormous until you think about the many ways in which we use spices. Think of all the prepared meats we eat — hot dogs, bologna, salami, pastrami, corned beef. It is the sharp spices in them that gives them the tangy taste that people love. Think of the pickles, mustard, ketchup, and dressings we use on our foods. They would give little flavor if they were not made with a mixture of many spices. Think of the cakes we bake and buy — apple pie, doughnuts, chocolate cake, gingerbread. Their mouth-watering flavors come from the allspice, cinnamon, nutmeg, and other spices baked into them. There is hardly a food you can name that does not contain some kind of spice.

And spices are important in other ways. Since earliest times, they have been used in medicines and drugs to numb pain and cure many kinds of ailments. Doctors still prescribe remedies made of spices, such as mustard plasters to treat chest colds, oil of cloves to relieve toothaches, and pills and cough medicines made with snappy spices that hide the bitter taste of the medicine. Oils that come from spices are also used in making perfumes. Especially important are oils from the bark of the cinnamon plant and from the seeds of cloves, nutmeg, and anise.

Like people in all periods of history, we depend on spices to give variety to our meals and to our lives.

COMMON SPICES

SPICE DEALERS and spice trade associations use the word "spices" in two different ways. Sometimes they mean the dried bark, root, fruit, or berry of plants that grow only in the tropics. In this sense, they call cinnamon, ginger, nutmeg, pepper, and other spices that originally came from tropical eastern lands "true spices."

More often, they use the word "spices" in a broader sense to mean many kinds of food seasonings that come from plants. In this sense, spices include (1) the true spices, (2) herbs — such as basil, chervil, marjoram, and sage — which come from the leaves of plants that grow in temperate climates, (3) seeds — such as caraway, mustard, poppy, and sesame — which are the seeds of plants that grow both in tropical and temperate zones, and (4) blended seasonings — such as chili powder and curry powder — which are blends of spices, herbs, and seeds.

The broader, more common meaning of the word "spices" is the one used here, and on the following pages you will find the most frequently used true spices, herbs, seeds, and blends described in alphabetical order according to their common names. The scientific name of the plant from which each spice comes appears in parentheses underneath the common name.

All the spices listed here can be bought in food stores. They come in small jars or cans, and are made up of dried parts of spice plants in either whole, ground, or crushed form. The best way to store spices is to keep them tightly sealed in a cool part of the kitchen, away from direct sunlight or heat. They should be checked regularly, and if their color is dull or their aroma weak, they should be replaced.

Many spices, such as basil, marjoram, mint, sage, and thyme, can be grown easily in a garden or as window plants. Once planted, they usually need little care. When grown, their leaves, stems, roots, or seeds can be used fresh or dried and ground into a powder. In cooking, generally, a half teaspoon of dried spice is equal to two teaspoons of the fresh spice.

Allspice
(Pimenta officinalis)

This spice gets its name from its taste, a combination of several other spices, especially cinnamon, cloves, and nutmeg. Actually, it is a single spice that comes from the fruit of an evergreen tree. The allspice tree grows only in the western hemisphere, mostly on the

island of Jamaica. Columbus saw the tree but did not realize that it bore a valuable spice. The Spaniards who came later thought the pea-size allspice berry was pepper. They named it *pimienta*, which means pepper. Gradually the name changed to *pimento*, and that is what the people of Jamaica still call allspice although it is not at all related to pepper.

To gather allspice, workers twist or cut off branches from the tree while the berries are still green and unripe. Then they spread the branches on canvas and beat them until all the berries fall off. The berries are dried in the sun for several days until they turn a dark reddish brown.

The dried allspice berry is used both whole and as a ground powder. It is an important seasoning for pickles and a favorite in making pot roast, mincemeat, and plum pudding.

Anise
(Pimpinella anisum)

Throughout history, the anise plant (pronounced *AN-is*) has been considered almost magical. At different times people believed that holding or eating parts of the plant could prevent indigestion, cure snakebite, guard against the evil eye, ward off nightmares, and stop epilepsy. Anise is mentioned in the Bible, and was a popular herb in ancient Rome.

Today, the licorice taste of the anise seed makes it an important seasoning in candy, cookies, cakes, and breads. It is also used in making absinthe and other alcoholic beverages. Anise leaves make good garnishes for salads and vegetables.

The anise plant is a small, annual one, related to the parsley family. It originated in Egypt and other countries near the Mediterranean Sea, and now grows in many lands. The United States imports about

five hundred tons of anise seed a year, much of it from Spain and Turkey.

Basil
(Ocimum basilicum)

In India, basil (pronounced *BAZ-ul*) is considered a sacred herb and is planted outside temples. In Italy, boys and girls regard it as a symbol of romance, and often wear basil leaves to show that they are in love. The ancient Greeks gave basil its name, which means "king," because they believed that it was the king of all herbs. The French still call it *herbe royale*, or royal herb.

32

This popular herb, also known as sweet basil, comes from an annual plant of the mint family. Its leaves are bright green and turn brown when dried. Most of the basil we buy is made up of the dried crushed leaves and stems of the basil plant.

The sweet, delicate flavor of basil makes it a delicious flavoring for tomato dishes, spaghetti sauce, soups, and stews. Fresh basil may be grown in a garden or a window pot, and its leaves chopped up and used for flavoring salads.

Basil originated in India and Iran, and is now grown in the United States, France, Hungary, and Belgium.

33

Bay Leaf
(Laurus nobilis)

An ancient Greek myth tells how the gods turned the beautiful nymph Daphne into a stately tree to help her escape the love of the god Apollo. Since Apollo could not have Daphne's love he made the tree sacred to himself.

The tree was the laurel, or sweet bay, and it held a special place in Greek life. Its branches were used to decorate the palaces of emperors, and its leaves were woven into wreaths to crown heroes, poets, and athletes. We still use the term "to win one's laurels," meaning to win honors.

The leaf of the laurel tree is called bay leaf or laurel leaf. It is shiny green, about three inches long, and has a strong flavor. Cooks use dried whole bay leaves to flavor stews, soups, and sauces. Food manufacturers use bay leaves in pickling and in making vinegar.

Most of the bay leaves we cook with are imported from Greece, Turkey, Portugal, and Yugoslavia.

Caraway Seed
(*Carum carvi*)

One of the oldest of spices is caraway seed, which probably origi-

nated in Asia Minor. More than two thousand years ago, Roman soldiers spread its use throughout Europe as they conquered land after land. During the Middle Ages, people considered caraway seeds good for stomach ailments. One medieval book also advised that caraway "restoreth hair where it has fallen away."

The seeds come from a plant of the parsley family which blooms every two years. Because the ripe seed shatters easily when it is dry, caraway seeds must be harvested at night or in the early morning hours before the sun rises.

Rye bread usually contains caraway seeds — actually it is this seed that gives the bread its distinctive taste. These curved brown seeds also add flavor to cheeses, soups, and pork and sauerkraut dishes. The United States gets most of its supply of caraway seeds from the Netherlands.

Cayenne Pepper
(Capsicum frutescens)

The "hottest" of all spices, cayenne comes from the dried ripe fruit, or pod, of a group of plants known as capsicums. These plants grow in tropical parts of America. Although the spices that come from the plants are called peppers, they are not related to ordinary white or black pepper.

Cayenne is sometimes called red pepper. It has a burnt-orange color and a strong, burning taste. Made from several kinds of capsicum peppers, it is almost always used in ground form. Most cayenne is produced in California, the Carolinas, and Louisiana.

This sharp spice is excellent with spaghetti, pizza, and other Italian dishes. But only a small amount at a time should be used.

Celery Seed
(*Apium graveolens*)

The munchy celery stalks we eat have little to do with the spice called celery seed. This spice is the dried fruit of the wild celery plant, known as smallage.

These light-brown seeds are so tiny that it takes more than 750,000 to make a pound. The seed may be used whole or in celery salt, which is a mixture of ground celery seed and table salt. Either way it makes a good seasoning for tomato juice, salad dressings, fish, potato salad, and egg dishes.

The United States imports most of its celery seed from France and India.

Chervil
(*Anthriscus cerefolium*)

The lacy, delicate leaves of this herb look and taste much like parsley. Either fresh or dried, it adds a pleasant taste to salads, sauces, and soups. The French often combine it with other herbs in a blend that they call *fines herbes*, or fine herbs. Much of the chervil used in the United States comes from France.

Chili Powder

Many Americans suddenly "discovered" chili powder during World War II, when Asian and European spices were hard to get. Until then, most persons had considered this Southwestern blend of spices too "hot" for them. The powder is a mixture of chili peppers from the capsicum family with cumin seed, oregano, and garlic powder. It has been used since the 1800's by people in Texas, Arizona, New Mexico, and other Southwestern states. Tradition says that an Englishman living in Texas invented chili powder when he was trying to imitate the curry powder he had tasted in India.

The most important use of chili powder is in chili con carne, made of ground beef, tomatoes, pepper, and kidney beans. This popular spice is also used in many Mexican-style dishes and in barbecue sauces, gravies, and stews.

Cinnamon
(*Cinnamomum cassia* or *Cinnamomum zeylanicum*)

For hundreds of years, this wonderful spice was one of the most sought-after and precious of the true spices. Its delightful taste and appetizing aroma make it a delicious addition to all sorts of cakes, cooked fruits, desserts, and candies.

The cinnamon we use is not the true cinnamon that is grown in Ceylon. Our cinnamon is cassia cinnamon, which is imported from South Vietnam and Indonesia. The Ceylon cinnamon, whose scientific name is *Cinnamomum zeylanicum*, is mild and light colored. Mexicans use a great deal of it, especially in chocolate drinks. Cassia cinnamon, or *Cinnamomum cassia*, has a rich reddish-brown color and a strong flavor.

Both kinds of cinnamon come from the bark of evergreen tree branches. The tops of the trees are cut off when the trees are young, and branches are grown from the tree stumps. Twice a year, workers cut the branches from the stumps and carefully peel off the bark. As the bark dries, it curls up. The workers place smaller rolls of bark into larger ones to form quills, which we call cinnamon sticks. Experts taste samples of the sticks and divide them according to their quality. Then the groups of cinnamon sticks are rolled into grass mats. Several mats are tied together to form large bales, and these are shipped to many parts of the world.

The dried cinnamon sticks may be sold whole or ground up. To make ground cinnamon, special machines first chop the cinnamon sticks into small pieces and then grind the pieces into a fine powder.

Cloves
(*Caryophyllus aromaticus*)

At one time, clove trees grew only in the Moluccas, or Spice Islands. The people there valued the clove tree so much that they planted one whenever a child was born. Parents believed that the tree was a symbol of the child's life. If it grew strong and sturdy, so would he.

Cloves are the dried, unopened buds of the clove tree. The name "clove" comes from a French word that means *nail*, because the dark-brown buds look like tiny nails. Most clove trees carry from thirty

thousand to fifty thousand buds, which are carefully handpicked just before they are ready to open. After they dry, the cloves have a wonderfully sweet, rich aroma. They may be used whole to flavor ham and pork and to pickle fruit. Ground cloves add a strong, sweet taste to baked goods, desserts, and sweet vegetables such as beets and sweet potatoes.

For years, cloves were among the most valuable and sought-after of all spices. After Europeans discovered clove trees in the Moluccas, they began planting them in other lands as well. Today, many of the world's finest cloves come from Madagascar and Zanzibar.

Coriander
(*Coriandrum sativum*)

The "hot-dog spice," coriander seed (pronounced *koh-rih-AN-dur*), is an important ingredient in frankfurters and sausages. Food manufacturers also use it in making curry powder and as a flavoring for cakes. Coriander leaves are sometimes called Chinese parsley and are used in many East European dishes.

Coriander has been known since earliest times. The Bible mentions that manna, the food eaten by the Israelites during their wanderings in the desert, was like coriander seed. The seed is small and light colored and has a mild, sweet taste. Most coriander comes from Argentina, France, Morocco, and Romania.

Cumin Seed
(Cuminum cyminum)

Under a microscope, the tiny cumin seed (pronounced *KUM-in*) looks like a small ear of corn. Its actual length ranges from about ⅛ of an inch to ¼ of an inch. The seed is yellowish brown and has a tangy taste that makes it an essential ingredient in chili powder and curry powder. Cumin seed comes from a plant that grows in such countries as Iran, Morocco, Syria, and Lebanon.

In ancient times, cumin was a symbol of greed and miserliness. Later it stood for faithfulness. In Germany, during the Middle Ages, brides and grooms often carried a little cumin seed with them during their marriage ceremony to make sure they would remain faithful.

Curry Powder

American curry powder tries to capture the flavor of the sharp curries, or special sauces, of India. The Indians, who invented curry, have dozens of different kinds, all made from freshly ground or pounded spices. Many Indian curries are so strong and "hot" that they make people perspire from eating them.

Ready-made curry powder combines as many as twenty spices, including cayenne, cloves, coriander, ginger, and turmeric. Favorite uses for it are in chicken, lamb, shrimp, and rice dishes. Hostesses often serve special side dishes, such as chutney, chopped raisins, and shredded coconut, to round out an elegant curry dinner.

Dill
(Anethum graveolens)

Through the ages, many magical beliefs have grown up about the dill plant. According to one old rhyme, dill could "hinder witches of their will." The ancient Greeks believed that holding dill in the left hand could prevent epilepsy. A medical book of the Middle Ages advised that a person would sleep well if he wore a sprig of dill to bed. And an early herbal (a book about herbs) claimed that dill "destroyeth the yexing" (hiccups).

Such wondrous powers are no longer attributed to this small plant of the parsley family. Today the most useful part of the plant is the seed, and its most important use is in the production of dill pickles.

The seed is small, tan in color, and tastes something like caraway seed. Some dill grows in the United States. Much of it is imported from India.

Fennel
(Foeniculum vulgare)

There was almost no limit to the medical cures that ancient peoples believed this herb could bring about. It could make people young, strong, and healthy. It could stop hiccups, cure coughing, and sharpen eyesight. It could even help fat people become thin again.

Nobody uses fennel in reducing diets today. But we do use the fennel seed, with its licoricelike taste, to flavor medicines and to add a good taste to apple pie and many kinds of cakes and breads. Manufacturers also use oil of fennel in making perfumes and cosmetics. The United States imports more than 300,000 pounds of fennel seeds a year, mostly from India and Argentina.

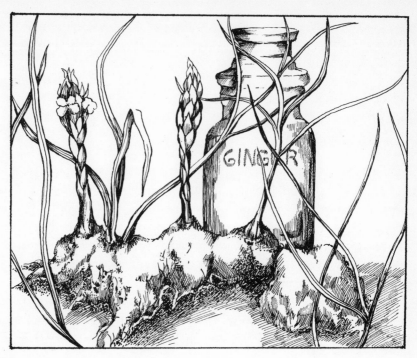

Ginger
(*Zingiber officinale*)

Can you imagine not having ginger ale, gingerbread, or gingersnaps?
These all-time favorites have been popular for so many years that we
never stop to think about where or how they began. Actually, ginger
was one of the first true eastern spices to be used in the West. Both
the ancient Greeks and Romans loved it and used it to make fancy
gingerbreads. For years during and after the Middle Ages, ginger
was so well liked and valued that only the richest people could afford
it. In England, during the 1500's, gingerbread was the special treat
at royal balls. Queen Elizabeth I had a baker whose main job was to
create gingerbread lords and ladies modeled after the queen's guests.

The ginger plant, native to the East Indies, was introduced in the

New World during the 1500's, and most of the finest ginger is now grown in the island of Jamaica in the British West Indies. The ginger we use as spice comes from the roots of the ginger plant. When the plant is about a year old, the roots are dug up. Then they are washed, dried, and bleached in the sun. The sun-bleached ginger has a light tan color. Jamaica ginger is usually peeled before it is dried. To peel the ginger, workers dip the roots in boiling water and then scrape off the peel with a knife.

We can buy ginger either whole, cracked (broken into pieces), or ground. Whole and cracked ginger are used to flavor syrups and pickling spice. Ground ginger is important in making ginger ale and baked goods.

Marjoram
(Majorana hortensis)

This delicate herb belongs to the mint family and is related to the

more popular oregano. Marjoram (pronounced *MAHR-joh-rum*) is used either as whole dried leaves or in ground form to flavor meats, fish, and vegetables. The marjoram plant originated in western Asia and the Mediterranean area, and now grows in many lands, including the United States.

Mint
(*Mentha spicata* and *Mentha piperita*)

There are many kinds of mint, but the most important kinds used as food flavorings are spearmint (*Mentha spicata*) and peppermint (*Mentha piperita*). Both flavorings are made from dried leaves of mint plants and both have a tangy yet somehow cool taste. There are dozens of uses for mint in the kitchen — in sauces for lamb, and in jellies, fruit salads, soups, green salads, and tea. Mint grows in Kentucky and along the west coast of the United States, and is also imported from Belgium, France, and Germany.

Mustard

(*Brassica alba* and *Brassica juncea*)

Tradition says that a housewife, Mrs. Clements of Durham, England, discovered the way to make mustard powder during the 1700's by crushing mustard seeds. Since then, the name Durham has come to stand for the finest of mustards. Mustard seeds were important, however, long before Mrs. Clements' day. The Chinese used them thousands of years ago, and Roman soldiers carried these seeds to every land they conquered. It was the Romans, in fact, who introduced mustard seeds into England.

51

Manufacturers use two kinds of mustard seeds, white or yellow ones and dark brown or "oriental" ones. Both come from annual plants of the mustard family. Stores sell mustard in three forms: (1) as whole seeds, (2) as mustard powder, and (3) as prepared mustard. Whole seeds are used in pickling and in flavoring salads. Powdered mustard is important in sauces and in spicing fish and meat. It has little taste until it is mixed with cold water. Prepared mustard, the most popular kind, is made of a mixture of ground seeds, spices, salt, and vinegar. It adds zest to cold meats, cheeses, and especially hot dogs.

Large amounts of mustard are grown in the United States. Mustard seeds are also imported from Great Britain, Canada, and Denmark.

Nutmeg and Mace
(Myristica fragrans)

These two spices come from the same fruit of a tall evergreen tree. Nutmeg is the pit, or seed, of the fruit, and mace is a bright-red, lacy covering that surrounds the pit. Both are used dried and either ground or whole to flavor baked goods, puddings, and desserts. Mace has a sharper flavor than the sweet, delicate nutmeg.

The nutmeg tree may grow as high as seventy feet. To gather the nutmegs, workers use long poles to which a basket and prongs are attached. The prongs loosen the fruit, which falls into the basket. To prepare the spices, the workers throw away the outer husk of the fruit and separate the mace from the nutmeg. Then they leave the nutmeg and mace to dry for several days.

Nutmeg and mace were among the most precious of the true spices eagerly sought by Europeans. For thousands of years, nutmeg

trees grew only in the Moluccas, in present-day Indonesia. Since the 1700's, they have been planted in many other lands. But we still get much of our finest nutmeg and mace from Indonesia.

Oregano
(Origanum spp.)

Until World War II, most American homemakers knew oregano (pronounced *uh-REG-uh-no*) only as a form of marjoram, and sweet marjoram or wild marjoram was the name used for this spicy

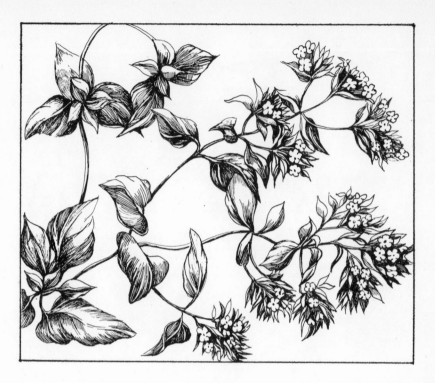

herb in most cookbooks. After the war, American GI's returned home raving about a wonderful Italian dish called pizza, and the herb oregano that flavored it. Within a short time oregano became one of the most popular of all spices. Each year its sales zoom higher and higher as people find more and more uses for it.

The herb is made of the dried leaves of a plant in the mint family. It is used whole, crushed, or ground, and has a taste similar to that of marjoram, only stronger. In fact, oregano is the Spanish name for marjoram. It is an excellent flavoring not only for pizza but also for many Spanish, Mexican, and Italian dishes.

Paprika
(*Capsicum annuum*)

This spice helped to win a Nobel Prize for a Hungarian scientist in 1937. Professor Albert Szent-Györgyi discovered that paprika contains certain substances that help keep the blood system healthy. For his experiments with it and other food products, he was awarded a Nobel Prize in Physiology and Medicine.

Paprika (pronounced *puh-PREE-kuh*) is made from the dried pods of capsicum peppers and is always used ground. It is bright red. American paprika has a very mild, sweet taste. Hungarian paprika is somewhat sharper and tangier. Both are used in making Hungarian goulash and in adding a tempting color to salads, eggs, vegetables, and broiled foods.

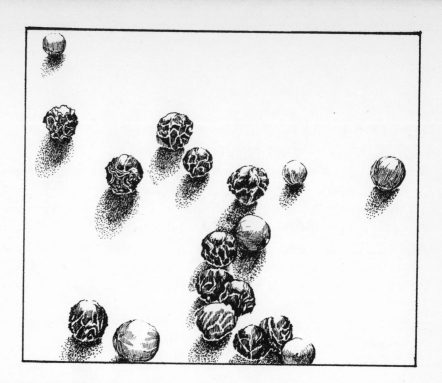

Pepper
(Piper nigrum)

The king of spices, pepper, has always been the world's most popular spice. Throughout ancient and medieval times, it was the most expensive and cherished of all spices because of its strong taste and its value in preserving meats. In many countries, it was used as money, carefully weighed and counted in paying rents, taxes, and dowries. It was the search for pepper, more than for any other spice, that led to the great explorations of the world during the Age of Discovery.

Both black and white pepper come from berries of a tropical vine. Black pepper is made from berries picked just before they ripen. The berries, which are red when picked, turn black and shrivel up as they dry. They are sold as whole peppercorns or in ground-up form. Many persons prefer to buy the whole peppercorns and to use

56

their own pepper grinders to get freshly ground pepper whenever they want it. White pepper is prepared from the completely ripe berry of the pepper vine. The berry is soaked in water soon after it is picked, and the outside covering is removed. The remaining kernel has a light, straw color. White pepper is sold only in ground form. It has a milder flavor than black pepper, which makes it more popular than black pepper in Europe and less popular in the United States.

The pepper vine grows only in tropical areas very close to the equator. The United States imports more than twenty-five thousand tons of pepper a year, most of it from India, Indonesia, Ceylon, and Brazil.

Poppy Seed
(Papaver somniferum)

These tiny blue seeds from the beautiful poppy plant are so small that 30,000 of them may fit into one pod and it takes more than 900,000 to make a pound. Although the plant from which these

seeds come is the same one that produces the drug opium, the seeds do not have any druglike properties.

The United States imports poppy seeds from the Netherlands, Denmark, Sweden, Poland, and Turkey. The seeds may be used whole as a topping for breads and rolls or crushed as a filling for cakes and pies. Melted butter mixed with poppy seeds makes a delicious dressing for noodles and rice.

Rosemary
(Rosmarinus officinalis)

The dried leaves of this herb look like little pine needles. They have a strong flavor and make a delicious spice for sprinkling on lamb, chicken, beef, and many kinds of salads. The rosemary shrub is a member of the mint family. It grows mostly in Spain, Portugal, and other Mediterranean countries, as well as in California.

Through the ages, rosemary has been given many symbolic meanings. Its most famous meaning comes from the words of Ophelia in Shakespeare's *Hamlet*: "There's rosemary, that's for remembrance."

Saffron
(Crocus sativus)

The world's most expensive spice, saffron (pronounced *SAF-run*), comes from the part of the purple crocus flower called the stigma. This is the part that collects pollen. It looks like a thin, delicate, yellow-orange thread. Each crocus flower has only three stigmas, and seventy-five thousand flowers must be gathered and handpicked to make a single pound of saffron. That is why this spice is so expensive.

Luckily, only a small amount of saffron need be used to add taste and color to meals. Just one or two strands of the dried stigmas give a rich yellow color and a delicate flavor to many foods — especially rice and chicken dishes. Most of the saffron used in the United States comes from Spain and Portugal.

Sage
(Salvia officinalis)

"Why should a man die while sage grows in his garden?" This was a popular saying during the Middle Ages, when people believed that sage could cure any number of illnesses. Even today, country people in many parts of Europe prepare sage tea to relieve headaches and colds.

In America, this herb is the most popular one used in making poultry stuffing and seasoning. It has a strong, fragrant odor and a slightly bitter taste. It is prepared from the dried leaves of a plant in the mint family, and may be bought whole, crushed, or ground. The

United States imports sage from Yugoslavia and other parts of southern Europe.

Savory
(Satureia hortensis)

This herb is a delicious flavoring for beans. In fact, the German word for savory means "bean herb." There are two kinds of savory — summer savory and winter savory. It is the dried leaf of summer savory that we usually use as a spice. Either whole or ground up, dried savory leaves add a good taste to poultry stuffing, meats, salads, and scrambled eggs. According to an old home remedy, a fresh savory leaf placed on a bee sting will quickly relieve the pain.

Most of the savory we use comes from France and Spain.

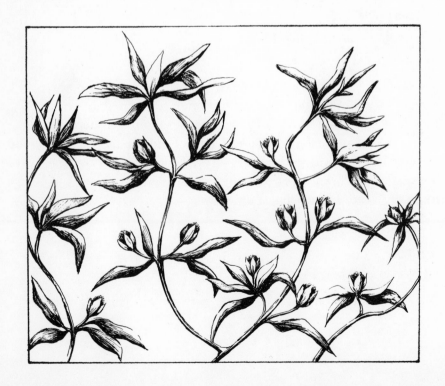

Tarragon
(*Artemisia dracunculus*)

This herb is best known as a flavoring for tarragon vinegar, an ingredient of French salad dressings. Tarragon is made of the dried, slender leaves of the tarragon plant, which originated in Siberia. The people of western Europe knew nothing about the herb until the 1200's, when an Arab physician living in Spain declared that it could sweeten the breath, put a person to sleep, and cover the taste of bitter medicine. Tarragon is grown in the United States and is also imported from France and Yugoslavia.

Thyme
(*Thymus vulgaris*)

New England clam chowder made with thyme (pronounced *time*) has been a traditional American dish for many years. This herb from the mint family is also used in stuffings and seafood dishes and as thyme butter for breads. Some homemakers serve honey flavored with thyme as a special delicacy. Thyme oil, called thymol, is an important ingredient in many cough drops.

The ancient Greeks considered it a special compliment to tell someone that he "smelled of thyme," because the herb has such a pleasant fragrance. During the Middle Ages, when ladies embroidered scarves for their knights, a popular design showed a bee flying over a sprig of thyme — a symbol of sweetness and courage.

Thyme is sold both as whole dried leaves and in ground form. It is imported from France, Portugal, and Spain.

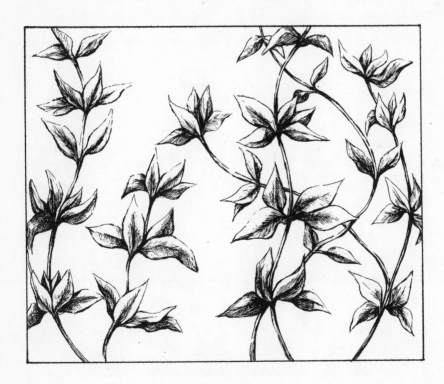

Turmeric
(*Curcuma longa*)

In the United States, turmeric (pronounced *TUR-mer-ic*) is known mostly as an ingredient in prepared mustard and in curry powder. But in Asia, it has many uses, as a spice, a dye, and a medicine. In many Asian countries, women use it as makeup. They dip their hands into water colored golden with turmeric and then rub their cheeks to give their skin a golden glow. In India, people mix turmeric with milk to form a soothing lotion which they apply to their eyes.

Like ginger, turmeric comes from the roots of a plant. The orange-yellow turmeric roots are cleaned, boiled in water, and then dried in an oven. They may be used whole or in ground form. The United States gets its turmeric from India, Jamaica, Haiti, and Peru.

IMPORTANT DATES IN SPICE HISTORY

1700's B.C. Joseph's brothers sell him into slavery to a caravan of spice merchants on their way to Egypt.

50 B.C. The Romans introduce mustard seed into England.

30 B.C. The Romans conquer Alexandria in Egypt and make it a chief spice port of the ancient world.

A.D. 410 Alaric, barbarian leader of the Visigoths, sacks Rome and demands three thousand pounds of peppercorns as a ransom.

1000's-1400's The city of Venice grows rich and powerful because of its trade in spices and other eastern goods.

1295 Marco Polo returns from China and describes the lands where spices grow.

1492 Columbus discovers America and believes it to be the rich spice lands of the Indies.

1498 Vasco da Gama finds the first all-water route to India and returns to Portugal laden with spices.

1522 Sebastián del Cano completes the voyage around the world begun by Ferdinand Magellan and brings back a treasure in spices.

1600's-1700's The Dutch and the English become rivals for control of the spice trade, with the English finally winning out.

1800's American sea merchants make daring pepper voyages to the island of Sumatra, becoming world leaders in the pepper trade.

1900's The United States becomes the major spice-trading country in the world.

1940's World War II cuts off supplies of many key spices to the United States. Native American chili powder grows in importance.

1960's The sale of all kinds of spices leaps to new heights in the United States.

INDEX